IN A FISHERMAN'S LANGUAGE

Fowler Road Press

49 Fowler Road
North Stonington, CT 06359
Telephone: 860-535-4413

ISBN 978-0-9821685-6-1

Third Edition Published February, 2012

Photograph of Men Marching in the first Blessing of the Fleet in Stonington, 1954.
Left to Right: Gino Rendeiro, Manny Aranjo, James Arruda Henry, Antone "Billy" Roderick

Printed in Canada

IN A FISHERMAN'S LANGUAGE

AN AUTOBIOGRAPHY BY
CAPTAIN JAMES ARRUDA HENRY

FYI...

In **A Fisherman's Language** was written by my grandfather, James Arruda Henry. I am the eldest of his five grandchildren and eleven great grandchildren. During the three summers which followed my High School graduation, I worked with my grandfather on his lobster boat as his only crew member.

On board the *Noranda*, I learned all about the dangers and rewards of lobstering. I also learned about the nature of the sea. But what was most endearing to me — and continues to be this very day — is that I found my grandfather to be an excellent story teller.

Pop is quick witted, precise and practical. He is socially active. His life has been about giving, to his family, to his friends, and the people of his town. He went to church, to town meetings, and was an integral part of the Fisherman's Association.

He appeared in featured articles for the newspaper, partaking in various community events, including the founding and establishment of the Blessing of the Fleet in Stonington,Ct.. He has a driver's license. He's owned and captained his own boats. He can navigate by day or night or in the thick of fog with or without the use of technology. He knows nearly as much about plumbing and carpentry as anybody in those trades. He even designed and built his own house.

When he lost his eldest daughter, my mother, to leukemia, my sister and I went across the street to live in his home. Pop always encouraged us to do well in school. He stressed the importance of a good education. It wasn't until my grandfather was in his mid nineties that he revealed his secret. For more than nine decades he was unable to read or write.

The collection of stories which follow is the result of his extraordinary journey into literacy, and the following selection of memories reflect his natural approach to storytelling.

With love, respect and gratitude,

Marlisa

Hank

I do not know how to put this down. I was going fishing with a three-man crew: me and my two cousins. Arthur, who we called Hank, was making his last trip. His brother, Marion, was going to take his place. We were about two hours southeast of Block Island. The weather was looking good. We set the net and towed about a half hour. I said, "Let's take up and see what's here."

The swell was getting bigger. Hank's job was to hold the towing cable down alongside the stern bit. I was in the wheelhouse. I turned the wheel a bit to the starboard, then I backed up to give him some slack. In the meantime, another swell came and the swell went up and then came down deeper than we expected. Hank was trying to hold the cable down but the swell was so big that the boat kept going down and the cable tightened as he hung in the air over the water.

Hank always did a goddamned good job. This time it was too goddam good. He hung onto that wire too long. I headed back to the wheelhouse to straighten out the boat. While I headed back, the boat swung around just enough so that Hank was still hanging over the water. Marion was in shock. Everything happened so fast. I heard Marion say "He's hanging over the water!" Marion was so shocked and shook up he could hardly get the words out. I tried to swing the boat around so that Hank would be hanging over the deck, but while I was doing that, he dropped into the water. He started swimming towards us. I was some surprised – I didn't think he could swim. So I called out "Keep swimming Hank, you're doing good – keep it up!" I grabbed the stern line and threw it to him, but he missed the line by an inch or two. The wind and the tide pulled him farther away from us. It wasn't too windy – it was just the tide and the swell. I was yanking my clothes off and told Marion how to put the boat in gear so that we could stay close to Hank. "If we get too far away, put the boat in gear, so we keep sight of him."

Looking back now, Marion was in a state of shock and I really don't know how we ever survived without ever talking about it. We never talked about it.

I asked Marion if he could see Hank . Hank went down in his yellow oilers and sou'wester , that familiar, yellow fisherman's hat. I asked, "You still see him Marion?"

"I see the sou'wester over there", he said. I saw it too, took the wheel and got the boat around alongside the sou'wester. The water was so clear I could see Hank but he was way down deep and getting smaller every second. I knew I wouldn't be able to hold my breath just to get to him, never mind coming up. He was so deep, he looked the size of a kid. We couldn't save him. Marion and I just stood there and watched him disappear.

I went to the phone and called Chick Crawick who was fishing not too far away from us. I asked him to give me a hand and make a tow to try to pick him up. But the Coast Guard called in and said "No sense doing that; he's too far gone now - you'll never find him."

Several months later, someone got a call that a skeleton of a man had been found, but nothing came of that and God only knows if it was Hank.
The Coast Guard advised us to go in because there were only two of us and we'd lost a man. We headed back and as we started home the fog shut in. Marion and I didn't say a single word.

I stayed in bed for a least three weeks. I just wanted to die myself. My wife kept telling me it wasn't my fault. I done the best I could to save him. Even Hank's brother-in-law came over and told me the same. I'm thankful that Marion was able to witness what he saw and tell how it really happened because otherwise I might not believe that I had done enough.

This has been the hardest story to tell because of all the tears behind it. I haven't got over it yet.

The Wave

The weather was hot. One of the boys said, "Hey, let's go swimming!" and we agreed. We went swimming but the water was rough. When a big wave came some of the boys knew to dive into the wave but I did not know. I had to dive into the wave but the wave knocked me down and rolled me ashore. I had so much sand in my eyes and nose my ears and mouth, the other boys took me into deeper water to wash the sand out.

Jail

When we got out of the ocean, we started walking back where we usually hung out by the jail. That's where we used to watch the American prisoners. At the time the American sailors were there, they'd hire a car and all get in and go around the streets. One of them had a gun. Some kids were chasing the car when a big dog came. One of the sailors tried to shoot the dog but shot the kid by mistake. There was a big stink over that of course. I was a little kid and I don't remember all the details but I know they went to jail and that's how come we used to go up to the jail all the time and we used to be talking to them. Some of the kids could speak a little bit of English and they'd talk back and forth with the sailors.

Then someone said "Let's go to the farm. Some fruit will go good right now." So off we went to my grandfather's place.

Grandfather's Place

There were all kinds of trees you could think of – apple, pear, peach and plum. My father also grew pineapples in the hothouse. He had two of them. After my grandfather died, my grandmother gave each of the boys a share. It was a big place and surrounding it was a stone wall so you couldn't get in there with the fruit. But on the wall it had some drains to let the water come out. We were so small we used to crawl through the drain, especially after swimming. We used to sneak up there and go in there and take apples, grapes and pineapples. My father noticed one pineapple was missing because the pineapples were perfectly lined up so you could see if one was missing.

My father yelled "Hey, someone stole one pineapple – I will kill him if I catch him!" He was some tough, I will tell you!

Businessman

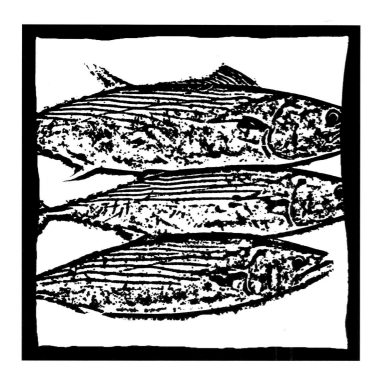

My father was a businessman. The house we lived in had a store. The store was on the first floor. You could get most anything you wanted in the store. We had a big door to let the big truck in to dump the salt. We had to make brine because we had two big cement tanks to put the fish in. When my father was told there was fish he would go down to buy the fish. He would have someone to take the fish up to the yard where the tanks were. Then the men would cut the fish into portions before we put the fish in the tanks. Before it went into the tanks, we put a good layer of salt on the bottom of the tank. Then we put fish, then more salt, then more fish until all the fish was down. Salt was used because there was no refrigeration in those days.

Sheep

When there was nothing else to do, or when things were slow, my father would take a trip to some island for a few days. When he came home, he brought back about 50 to 75 sheep.

The sheep stayed in the backyard. Each one of us kids took one sheep and we said, "That's mine." And we tied a piece of ribbon or something around the neck just so each one would know which was his. We were warned not to get too close to our pet sheep because they might "run away." My father had someone take about six sheep at a time to sell. The man went from town to town. If the man sold the six in one day, the next time he took more sheep. And that was his job, to sell sheep. I knew he could sell because he went to a different location to sell more sheep.

The Cobbler

When I was a little boy, we used to go around bare-footed. And we used to have our toes pretty well banged up. Finally, my father bought some leather. He had a cobbler come to the house to make shoes. My father bought more leather to make shoes. But at that time I did not know we were going to America or when we were going to America. My mother happened to come out of one of the rooms and saw him putting the leather around his body. She watched him and he tied it up, he was going to steal it. So she told him look she said if my husband catches you he will kill you and I know he will, you better put that leather back. He knows how much leather he bought and he knows how many shoes he could get out of that leather and finally he gave in and he put the leather back and he made all the shoes.

Manuel in World War I

I think when I came over here I was about six, seven I'm not sure. I can remember my mother getting a letter from my brother – it was written in English my mother couldn't read English so she had a friend of hers read it and I was sitting alongside of her but I didn't know what they were talking about because she was reading the letter to him. Manuel was out of the war and he was happy to get out of the war. Things like that there I can remember.

Coming to America

When we were ready to go to America we had to go by a small boat to get to the ship. Maybe the harbor in Ponta Delgada wasn't deep enough, for the ship was outside the harbor. To get all the people aboard, the tender made several trips. Before we got underway we were told where to go to our quarters. Although they were cargo bays, we had to sleep in them.

We got into some heavy weather, what they called heavy weather. The ship would go high and then go down low and the water would come right over the bow and then at the beginning there was a few kids that didn't do anything until one of us realized why that was. And we started playing and every time the boat would go up we'd run up midship as the water ran out of the scuppers, but when the boat went down the water came over the bow because it was real rough. We'd run as fast as we could to get back where we were safe. We weren't worried. We kept playing the game and running up and down until one time the skipper or whoever came over and stopped this because it was too dangerous and they locked us up when it was rough in the cargo bays. That's where we slept. We had straw for our beds and stuff like that and that's where we stood. We wasn't allowed to go on deck because they were afraid they were going to lose us. What about food? That there I don't remember one thing about. But I know we had to eat something. In those days a piece of bread, a piece of cheese, that was a big meal, it's the truth. A lot of people got hired by different people that had a lot of farming to do and they'd go out to their home and dig the dirt up around their plants and stuff and they used to bring their meals…a piece of cheese and a piece of cornbread, usually.

Landing in New York

They told us to come up and we jumped on the dock. It was very easy to get on the dock. We walked up and my brother was waiting for us there. And then of course we helloed and helloed and everything and we hugged one another (I´d never seen Manuel before). I was born in Boston, my father worked there. I was born there and I've got the papers to prove it. From Boston he wanted to go back to Portugal. His family was there at the time and of course I was only a little baby. My mother always wanted it but my brother was in the war here in the United States. Once he was out of the war and was working and everything he wanted to go to Portugal but he was afraid if he went to Portugal – Portugal was still at war – he would go to war because he was born in Portugal. He's the only one that was born in Portugal and all the rest of us was born here.

I don't know how many times my father's family came back and forth – course he had a good business in Portugal and he was making money – spending a lot of money though and while he come over here it was a different story.

Frank and James

We lived in a four family tenement in Bristol, R. I. My brother Frank and I took the horse and wagon at least twice a week to pick up garbage. We would go to people's yards to pick up their garbage. Most of the cans were below ground. I dumped their garbage into my can. That would save me from coming back. We took the wagon up to the pig farm. I said to my brother I was going to talk to the horse.

"About what?"

"A ride." I put my hand on his neck and rubbed it And I said "I know we worked hard today but we still got a long walk to get home. But if you give Frank and me a ride I will give you two quarts of oats."

And I said, "Frank, you are first."

"Oh no, you go first. "

I said, "OK." I got on. Then Frank got on. From now on we will ride because the wagon stays there so they can feed the pigs.

One day the wagon was free and we got the horse and wagon. We went to clean the people's backyard. We got one dollar for every load we took to the dump. We made twenty dollars. But I don't remember how long it took to make one dump run. If the houses were close we could make five dumps a day.

We were just about to put the horse in the barn. My father came with a friend. My father said to my brother Frank, "Did he pay you?"

"Yes, he paid me twenty dollars."

"Give it to me."

"I gave it to you."

My father took the horsewhip and he was whipping him.

His friend said, "Look in your pocket and see if the money is there."

The money was there. He was drunk. I know he was drunk. A good father would never do anything like that. What makes me feel bad is that I did not say one word. I knew he would whip me too.

The Bakery

We were in the bakery shop working there. When I got out of school I'd go down there and help them. One day I was just sweeping up and stuff like that – when finally Tommy, who with the father used to go around peddling the bread said, "Why don't you help bake bread?"

"I don't know how to make it."

"I'll show you."

So he taught me how to make the bread. Gee, and I was happy as hell and I was running like hell home to tell my mother that I was going to the bakery. I was about nine, somewhere in that neighborhood. And I'd make the bread. At first I had to make them round and they'd put them on a big wooden thing there and then they'd put the cover over it, towels over it to let it heat. And then they'd make bread – I know the names: Sicilian bread – three slices almost to the end, and then Vienna bread which was one slice across when the bread opens up. I could do that – I learned how to do that, but putting it in the oven, the big boys done it.

They had a hell of a big oven – that oven I guess was almost as wide as this room. And he had a long handle when he made the bread, you know? Of course when you're a kid it looks big – it's not as big as you think it was, but to me, that's what it looked like. It was a good-sized bakery. Then he put the wood in the fire until he got it to the correct temperature and then that's when the oven was ready: Then he goes and puts the bread in. And of course I never got paid or anything, I didn't want no money, I was helping, but he said take all the bread you want. I used to take home four or five loaves sometimes, but we used to eat a lot of bread. I enjoyed working there and everything. And that's when I use to go around with the father and the son. The mother couldn't speak a word of English – I learned Italian, a little you know, but she could understand me and I could understand her after a while. The father spoke very little English.

One day I said to the father, "I make bread, yes?" The father said, "No. We go bring bread to their houses. You take one bread give it to that house, first floor. Give this house the big round bread."

The woman said, "Take this bread back – this bread is hard. I like to get a fresh bread."

The father said, "Give me that bread." He put the bread on the seat and sat on the bread and went up and down two or three times. And he said, "Now, give the nice lady the nice fresh bread." Gee, I was happy as hell 'til my father took me out of there when we went to make cement blocks.

CEMENT BLOCKS

My father gave me a job making cement blocks. He told me where to go. Someone will be there to show that you have everything you need. So I made block after block for a long time – at least two weeks. From there I went to work where my father and the other men were working on a new house. The boss taught me how to run the cement mixer. My father and about five other men had wheelbarrows. I put sand-cement-water into the mixer. When it was mixed I put some in each wheelbarrow. They will dump it into the foundation of the new house that we are working on. Every man will dump his wheelbarrow of cement into the foundation. When the foundation gets to the right height, then we will go with cement block. We then will know what we can do for them and that is when I knew that my father got the job through his boss and then I was told how much money we were getting . The men got 50 cents an hour. I got 55 an hour! Every payday he gave me 50 cents to spend.

But on the Fourth of July my father gave me one dollar to spend. I was so happy that I went straight to the ice cream parlor. I got a glass of milk, a piece of apple pie, a dish of ice cream. After I finished eating I had just enough money to buy a small pack of firecrackers. I lit one and they all went off! I started to cry. I didn't have any more money.

Buying Corn

Years later in Bristol, RI we were in my brother Marion's house playing cards and drinking coffee and my father was in a good mood. Then Marion said, "Hey Par, do you remember when you called John names for not bringing any corn? Remember the way you'd say 'That brother of yours never brings corn home' Do you know why he never brought any corn?"

"No" my father said, "I don't know why he didn't."

"John didn't have enough money."

"What do you mean, 'John didn't have enough money?' I gave him the same amount as I gave you."

"Neither you nor John knew that I used to go in the cash register before I went for the corn and I used to take some money out because I knew that the corn was expensive and you wasn't giving us enough money so I turned around and took a few dollars more to make sure when I came to the first farm I'd get it and come right home and that's why I used to come back with the corn and John didn't have enough money – he couldn't come back with the corn."

In order to make the cornbread we had to go and buy the corn and take it to be ground into corn flour. On days there was no wind we'd leave our bag of corn there until the wind came back and they had a chance to grind the corn. Everything including cornbread was cooked in my mother's oven. I can't remember if we had a stove to make coffee – I know we drank a lot of coffee. I can remember having coffee with my mother as a little boy.

After Marion told his story that day so many years later, Par said "You son of a gun – I knew you were smart," he said, "I didn't think you was that smart." If Marion did it, it was okay by Par. And Marion sometimes got credit for more than he deserved because he was my father's favorite. One time Marion decided to kill a bull which was waiting in our yard to go to the slaughter house the next day. He couldn't wait. John didn't want any part of it, but he held the rope and may have calmed the animal by petting it. Suddenly Marion drove a ten inch knife right between the horns and the steer died instantly. But Marion didn't know anything more about butchering. It was John who told him he had to bleed the animal. And Marion said, "No, you don't have to do it." So John took the knife and slit its throat.

My father came up and asked, "What happened?" John and Marion had left by then, so I explained that Marion had killed the bull and thought he was all done. Even after I told him that John had done the bleeding, my father said something like, "That Marion is quite a man!"

Fort Wright

I was looking for a job and after two or three weeks I could not find a job. So I joined the National Guard, Battery C, in Bristol, R. I. Every week we would spend one day learning how to drill and salute the officers. Some of us did not know how to salute an officer and other officials. So we had to learn a lot more. We had to go to Fisher's Island within two weeks. All R. I. National Guard go to Fisher's Island for two weeks. Most all National Guard parade every day. Manuel Lewis was picked to teach us how to march and salute officers. Every time we went by one another, we would salute each other and laugh. Ha! Ha! We were having fun. We would salute anyone who came by. The sergeant came to tell us who we should salute. All of us started to salute the sergeant. "I thank you, but you do not have to salute me! Ha! Ha! Ha!"

Then the captain came. "What are you guys doing? You know we go to Fisher's Island in two weeks – so settle down!"

After we learned to salute, someone came and asked, "If you would like to go on the boat that tows the target, we need volunteers." I was one of eight that volunteered. When it was time to go we had to be at the dock where the boat was. We brought the target close to the boat and tied it. The experienced men retied the target to the boat with the correct amount of line. Then we went south of Fisher's Island. When we got to where we should be then the flag will go up. Now the boat will go east – how long, I do not know. Then we go west – how long I do not know. But the man in the wheelhouse will know. But I know the flag is up on land. So the battery will be shooting at the target. Then there will be another battery firing at the target. Then the next battery will shoot at the target. The only thing we didn't know is which battery was shooting at the target as they shot in turn. We didn't know how many batteries were shooting from Ft. Wright. Each shot was recorded, which battery shot it, and how close the shot came to the target. That's as close as I can remember about the true facts.

One of the batteries shot too close to the boat, so they pulled the flag down and ceased firing.

Lobstering

After my mother died, we stayed in the same house for about one year. My father then decided to go to Stonington, Connecticut. Some of his family still lived there. I was still in the National Guard, working in the red mill right by the state armory in Bristol, Rhode Island. My brother, Manuel, was working for The U. S. Rubber Company in Bristol until he was transferred to Naugatuck, Connecticut. His wife had family still living in Bristol, so they would stop in Stonington to see my father along the way to their visit.

They also visited me. They told me that Par had been lobstering for about one year and that he would like to have me come and help him. I went to the captain in the National Guard and told him that my father would like to have me help him. The captain said he would see what he could do for me and let me know.

I got an honorable discharge and went to work with my father for about one year. He talked down to me as if I was the little boy he once knew. My father was an alcoholic and didn't care for anyone but himself. For instance, he'd get a job from someone for him to do, but he would get me to do the job. Then when it was time to get paid, he'd ask me if I got paid and I said yes, he'd say, "Give me the money." That was his strategy, to get me to do his job and then take the money for himself.

One day I told him that the lobster pots by the breakwater needed bait and I was going to haul them. I went on my way. The weather was nice when I started rowing but after five to ten minutes it seemed like it was getting worse. The wind was from the west and it was blowing fairly well. I figured I couldn't get out to haul those pots, so I went to the westward to see if it would calm down. I went right to shore to be in the lee of the wind because the land was higher than the water. There was a big shed there and I went behind the shed to get away from the wind.

While I was behind the shed, I saw my father on a small motor boat with two or three guys all together there with him. They were going out to the breakwater to look for me, but the farther they got out, the weather got worse, so they turned around because they didn't see any dory. They were too far away from me to hear me when I yelled to them. They thought something was wrong like I must have drowned. Now I don't know how long I stood there but I realized I couldn't haul those pots so I went back home in fair wind. There was no problem there.

When I finally got back home, my father never said a word to me. I said, "You could at least say 'I am glad to see you - I thought you had drowned."

To anyone who has a son, please do not let this happen to your son. A good father would like to see his son go to school to at least learn to read and write. It means so much through life. I know that because I never had the chance to learn to read and write.

Manny's Shack

When I got away from my father, I went down to the dock to see Manny Piver. He was a R. I. lobsterman and could fish in New York water just like me. He had a shack at the dock in Stonington. I said, "I would like to sleep in your shack for a few days." He said, "OK by me." The first night I slept on oak boards. The next day someone brought a big cardboard box. That was my mattress.

Manny asked, "Would you like to come fish with me?"

"I would love to but on bad days if we come in early, I would like to train to fight." I must have been about twenty years old then, I'm not sure. There was a bunch of us just fooling around back then on Hancock Street just for fun, boxing, throwing a few punches. I got interested in fighting and started to run. John

Freitas was a lot younger than me. He used to give up a lot, but I kept running. We fought in Norwich in the state armory. We each got scheduled to fight. I fought a black man. He was tough. I could never knock him hard enough to fall – and I took a few good punches as well. But I was well trained and I won that fight.

John fought some amateur we didn't know. This guy was real good but he didn't want to go professional because he wanted to stay where he was and win more often. He wanted more credits. This amateur was hitting John so many times that John was getting madder by the minute. The other fella was dancing around and he tripped. Well, John goes down and starts punching him while he was lying on the floor. I can see that poor bastard now! The crowd started to roar. John gave himself away then. Everybody knew then that John didn't know how to fight. Boy, did that crowd roar!

I told Manny, "You never know when someone needs to get someone to fight at the very last minute. They got to fill the card. They will lie to you about who you will fight to get you to fill that card for them. It's happened to me four times already."

The first time that happened it was the first fight I had. I told the promoter I couldn't fight because I didn't have time to train. I was lobstering.

The promoter lied all the way through, telling me the man that he wanted me to fight was John Macioni, a nobody. He said the guy didn't know how to fight. He wasn't thinking about me at all. He was out just for himself. I knew he was lying and told him so. I felt sorry for the promoter so I did it to help him. If I could win, I could get more chances to fight. I lost that first fight.

After that fight, the promoter came to me twice more to fight John Macioni because he couldn't get anyone else to fight him. Like a damn fool I agreed to fight again and that made three fights I lost to John Macioni with no training. He asked me once more to fight. I didn't want to trust him at all, but like a damn fool I was looking to make a few dollars.

So I asked the promoter, "So, who do you have this time?"

"I would like you to fight Joe Devens."

Joe Devens had a good record. He had three knockouts in a row. "How much time do I have to train before the fight?" I think he told me two weeks – plenty of time to train. A long time before we fought, Joe had trained with us a few times. I had trained for a while at Joe Enos's Stonington pool hall where Joe Devens trained with us a couple of times before he went to Westerly where he met some guys he practiced with there. I stayed in Stonington because Joe Enos was still there. After Joe Enos went to New London, he was still my manager but I stood mostly on my own.

I couldn't find a sparring partner until I met Manny "Pig-Iron" Rose. We trained for the fight with Joe Devens. But Pig-Iron complained that I wasn't hitting hard enough. In fact, he wouldn't go to the fight because he was sure I would lose to Joe. Joe kept telling my friends to tell me not to fight him because he had to knock me out . Every time someone told me that, I'd run a few extra miles.

We went three or four rounds, I think. That was the number you fought back then, but they had to stop the fight because I was hitting him so much they were afraid I would hurt him. All my friends that were there jumped into the ring and carried me out of the ring. That was the part that really got me! I felt so good. The owner of the Greek restaurant came up to me. He spoke like a Greek, he said, "When you get cleaned up, come and see me. I got a big steak for you on the house!"

Before my very last fight, I was weighing in and getting looked over. The doctor took a look at me and asked, "What are you doing here?"

"I came to fight a nobody." The doctor told me, "What? Are you crazy?! You will be fighting the main bout! This guy is good."

So I went to see the promoter and I told him, "The doctor told me this man I'm supposed to fight is good. You told me he wasn't any good. Now what am I supposed to do? I haven't had any training."

"Oh," he says, "Just go in there and lie down if you have to."

This was killing me. I wanted to fight but I didn't want to fight. I thought about this for a long time. I asked myself, "What should I do? I have no money. I live in a shack. I'm sleeping on oak boards." If I won, I could win some money, but if I lost, I could get hurt and couldn't see a doctor. If I at least went in the ring, I could get paid. I decided to lie down.

We stepped around a few times and threw a few punches and then the guy swung one real close, but he missed me. I figured this was my time, so I lay down. They counted me out, and when we were all dressed up, ready to go home, we were in the hall of the arena when the fighter came to me and asked, "Did I hurt you much?"

There were kids all around watching us. I said to him, "I think you know you didn't even hit me. That was close, but I lay down because I had to."

He just looked at me. He didn't say a word. The kids just stood there with their mouths open. They couldn't believe what they heard. I was so ashamed of what I done that I never said a word about it to anyone until the day the fishermen gave me an honorary dinner at the Portuguese Holy Ghost Society Hall. I was 95 years old then.

I was giving a little speech. "I feel very honored to be here and I really appreciate it. I'm not a liar and I don't want to live with this lie that I'm about to tell you. "Every time I talk to someone about fighting, they would ask me,

'Did you like fighting?'

'Yes, I did.'

'How come you gave it up?'

My answer was, "I loved the women more than I used to love to fight. I know you may not believe this, but the real reason I quit fighting (because I did love fighting more than I loved women) was because I lay down during that last fight."

I knew I never should have lain down. That was the biggest mistake I ever made. I never should have lain down! But what else could I have done? I couldn't afford to get hurt.

Driver's License

My name is James Arruda, but I am incognito. I go by the name of James Henry. When I wanted to get my driver's license, I went down to Shannon's Garage. The officer came there for one day once a month to check them out. Mr. Shannon gave me an application for a license. I put my name down but that was all I could do. I got up to ask Mr. Shannon what else I had to do because I couldn't read the paper. When I got up, I happened to bump into the inspector. He asked me, "Who are you?"

Mr. Shannon said, "You mean to tell me you don't know Jimmy Henry, 'The Short Lobster King'?"

He took my unfinished application and said, "Let's go out for a road test." I drove good.

"You're OK." the inspector said. That's all I had to do to get my license.

Aboard *Geneve*

I was fishing on Billy Roderick's father's boat, the *Geneve*. We were a crew of four. We were just about to start to get ready to set the net, Someone yelled, "Fire in the engine room!"

Three of us each grabbed a fire extinguisher but I grabbed an air horn by mistake because I was so excited trying to do my best to put that fire out.

Sammy shouted at me, "Take that goddam air horn out of here! All you are doing is making the flames go higher!" I passed old man Roderick buckets of water and we all finally put that fire out. We cleaned everything up the best we could and then started fishing.

It took three men to set the seine net. I rowed the dory. Sammy was at the stern putting down the heavy part of the net with the rings to sink the net.

Billy was at the bow setting the topline with the corks to float the net and keep it open. Billy's father stayed in the big boat and used a long pole to help submerge the topline underneath the keel. Once it's underneath the keel we let the wind and the tide do the rest to get the boat over the seine. Sammy and Billy pursed the bottom ropes to close the bottom of the net. When you do that the two top lines will close as they go along. When they get the net in as close as they can, they use a scoop net to scoop the catch up and into the big boat.

On the way to the dock we talked about the fire. None of us knew what caused it, but we suspected that one of the wires hit metal and sparked a flame. Boy, did we laugh about that air horn! It was a big joke after that.

Oh, that Sammy was some joker! He was a clown, that's what he was. He used to roll his eyelids up and wore a big hat and overcoat. He'd have everybody on the uproar, laughing and everything.

When TV first came out, Sammy went to New York to take fish out. In those days you could only see TV in New York. Sammy was asked to be on TV. He was one of the first ones I knew that was on TV. I wonder if he rolled up his eyelids? I wouldn't be surprised.

Jitterbug

Before I got married, I was with Jimmy Sousa. Jimmy worked for the Stonington Boat Yard. They built fishing boats. Jimmy did most of the fine cabin work, lockers, tables, and wheelhouse work. Jimmy said to me,

"Why don't you build a boat?" I told him I didn't have that kind of money. I couldn't afford a big boat like that.

Jimmy said, "Why don't you build a small boat then?"

"I don't know how to build a boat."

"If you want to build one, I will help you."

So I agreed to build a small boat. That was the *JITTERBUG*. I used to do a lot of dancing so I imagined I named the boat *JITTERBUG* because of that. I used the boat for taking people out on fishing parties. I also used it for pleasure.

I used to let someone steer us around the harbor while I took Joey Kessler, the small one, up on my shoulder while his brother was in back of me on the surfboard. Boy, we used to go all over like that! I didn't want to sell the boat, but I wanted to get married so I sold the boat to pay for all the expenses.

When I was about 29 I married Jean Amato on September 27, 1942 at St. Patrick's Cathedral in Norwich. We moved to Stonington Borough with all the rich people. Our daughters, Noreen and Sandra, were born there.

I am some surprised that they have an instrument now that they call the Jitterbug. I would love to know whether whoever named it had anything to do with my boat.

Flying Lessons

When I was about 26 years- old I went to the airport in Stonington and said I would like to learn to fly. He said, "You came to the right place. We have the plane and we have the pilot. The plane is for two – the pilot and the learner. The pilot's job is to teach you how to take off, fly the plane and land it. His job is to explain everything to you before you take off." After he explained everything, I felt sure I understood what he said and I told him that. I don't remember just how many hours we practiced for, but he thought I was ready to give it a try.

I thought I was ready and so we went up. Once we got up there, he told me go a distance and circle around so I could get the idea of working the plane. I don't know how long we were up there, but he decided I should learn to land

and take off. So we tried the landing. When you land a plane you have to come in at a certain speed and I don't remember what the speed was. But the airport we landed at was north of the railroad tracks. It is not too big of an airport and has a short landing strip. He tries to explain to me that I had to come in at a certain angle to be sure we had enough room to land. As you go along it gets more complicated. It all depends on how hard you come in and how hard you hit. If you hit hard you are going to bounce and sometimes you can't control it and you have to go up and make another try. If you hit hard on one wheel it will throw the plane off balance and if you are not acquainted with these things you're in trouble! You've got to go up again and get back at a good enough point to navigate the plane . When I was landing, I came in like he said but I hit a little too hard on the wheel and the plane bounced, hit the other wheel, then went back again. We had to go up and he grabbed the the stick and took over and circled a bit.

He said, "I thought you were ready the way you talked and everything, but you can't learn everything in one try." So he landed the plane that time.

The next time I went back I asked my girlfriend, Jean, if she wanted to go up for a ride in the plane. We didn't take the learner's plane because we had three. So we took the passenger plane, a small plane that carried the pilot and three or four passengers. The three of us went up for a pleasant ride when I decided to put a little scare in Jean. I motioned to the pilot to do a few tricks before we came down. On the way home in the car I asked her how she liked it. She said, "It wasn't bad, but it is not for me!" Then she said I could either have her or the plane but not the two. I chose Jean.

I had paid for my lessons ahead of time because I never knew how much money I was going to make fishing and I wanted to make sure I had enough money to fly solo. I went back and told him the flying was over. I wanted the girl. He told me I still had money left and asked me if I still wanted the money or if I wanted to go up. We went up. We were flying around when he went up to do a stall. I think that's what they call it. He went real high up , pointed the nose down. made three spins and then pulled out. He said, "How do you like that?" I said, "Beautiful. I love it!"

"You want to try it?"

I said, "Yes." He told me what to do. You go up the right altitude and I don't remember how high. You hold the stick right close to your belly and don't let it go because the wind will try to take it out of your hands, You put your foot on the right pedal and the plane comes to a stall and takes a slow dive and spins.

He didn't tell me three spins, but he went three. When I did it, I went five. He told me not to let go of that stick because the wind would try to take it so I held on real tight. That stick was vibrating but I wouldn't let go. He suddenly yelled so loud that I got scared and let go of the stick.

He took over and landed the plane. We were walking away from the plane. My friends who were there at the airport, asked the pilot who was walking way ahead of me, "What happened?"

"That crazy son-of-a-bitch Jimmy Henry tried to kill me!"

I heard him say that and I said, "Hey wait a minute, what do you mean I tried to kill you?"

"Okay, okay it's my fault, I forgot to tell you to pull out after three spins."

One Good Tow

Don Crawford has fished with me before and we were in Martha's Vineyard and looking to make one tow for scup. The price of fish was good and I said if we could make one good tow we'd have a good week's pay. But sometimes we'd get into a hang. We do not know what's down there but if you hit a hang you will rip your net and I ripped three nets in a row trying to make that one tow. Crawford knew if we fixed that one net we would have a chance to make a trip. That's what I had: three nets. Out of the three nets I decided if I wanted to make another tow I would have to take twine from two of the nets to repair the third one.

The crew wanted to lie down and sleep but Crawford stood with me, filling up the needles for me with twine and I was cutting from one and patching where needed and mending it - I got the net fixed up just in time to put it overboard so we can make that one tow I was looking for. The other guys come up, "Hah! You want to waste some time – you're gonna rip this one too." They had no goddam faith in me, you know?

"Well," I says, "you may be right but you ain't changing my mind – I'm going to make a tow even if I have to do it alone!" And finally they decided to set the net and everything like I told them. We set the net. I'm not sure how long - I think we towed for a half hour - we usually go an hour or hour and a half - in a half hour I would know if I ripped up or if I was all right.

When they brought the goddam net in, the cod end is up and the front part where all the heavy stuff is still down in the water – the chain and everything.

Then they yelled, "Hey we got 'em! – We got 'em!"

"You sons of bitches you got 'em – who got 'em?"

And then, "Good thing we made another tow. "

I says, "Where's all these we's when we was mending and Crawford was holding the twine – at least Crawford stood out with me – you guys didn't – I should take half of your money."

"Oh no, you can't do that!"

I said, "I could if I wanted to but I won't."

They didn't want to work, they wanted to sleep. I was real tough in that respect. But I gave in. We went to New Bedford – took the fish out and everything. Normally, we'd take our trip to Stonington's fish buyer, but we talked it over and decided to sell the fish in New Bedford because we were closer to New Bedford and we'd get a good price there. Every time I went to New Bedford, I'd go to Aiello's, the fish buyer. He liked my fish, paid high market price nine times out of ten.

You put your fish weight on the auction boards. Now the fish buyers bid on the fish until they decide to sell and the highest bidder buys the fish. Mr. Aiello told me not to worry; he'd give me the price of the auction board.. And then finally we made a good week's pay out of that.

We'd get our check right away just as we would in Stonington, and we could clean the boat on the way home. Once we were in Stonington, all we had to do was tie up the boat and go home. The only things left to clean up were ourselves if we wanted peace and quiet - or anything else! - from our wives…

Pinched Nerve

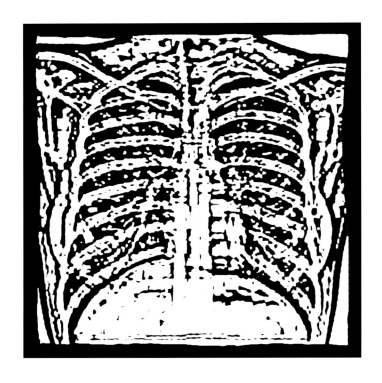

I came in from fishing one day and I had a terrific pain in my right shoulder. We called up Dr. Jones. He had two offices, one in New London and in Westerly, near the hospital. I went to him first in New London and he gave me a shot of cortisone. I felt real good – until the next morning. I had the same pain. I called him up and he said to come on up again.

I went back two more times. He asked me to show him where the pain was. He pressed certain spots along my arm with his finger and each time it hurt. He marked the spot and then put a needle to it. Those two times I felt great again until the next morning. The fourth time I saw him he said he had an idea what the problem could be but he wasn't sure. He wanted to have to have an X-ray taken to be sure. He told me he was going to draw me a diagram of what he thought the problem was and he would hold it up next to the X-ray to see if it matches.

Before the X-ray he had four needles hanging on me. The nurse came to take me to the X-ray and she saw the needles. She was shocked to see so many needles and gave out a scream!

We took the X-ray. Dr. Jones told me to sit and relax while we waited for the X-ray. When it came out, he put it down on the table and put his diagram next to it. He was right. It was a pinched nerve and I needed an operation.
I've always had a lot of respect for Dr. Jones. At that time I didn't think there were many doctors who would admit they were lower than another doctor. But when Dr. Jones told me he wanted his partner, Dr. Elliot, to do the operation because Dr. Elliot had learned to do this kind of operation from the man who invented this operation. I thought Dr. Jones was a real man and I had even more respect for him.

We became buddies. I appreciated him so much because it seemed like he could always make a place for me when I really needed it. Most every time I came in from fishing, I would clean a few cod fish – nice and fresh –and bring him the fillets. I've been operated on so many times I'd be lying if I told you how many times it was. Dr. Jones did most of them.

Once he invited me to go to the Lawrence and Memorial Hospital to display the incisions he had made. Once after I had come in from fishing, I'd gone home and cleaned up, then went to bring him the fish. He was working outside when I got there."Hey, Dr. Jones, I got some nice fresh codfish for you!"

"And I thank you and we'll enjoy it." We talked for a while and then he said. "Hey, come on upstairs – I want to show you something." He opened the door. There was a pool table. "I've got to have something to do. I've gotta learn to shoot pool. Can you shoot pool?"

"I can shoot pool, but I'm not that good."

He looked at me kind of funny like he wasn't sure I was tellin' the truth. We started shooting and had most of the balls off the table, when I put the stick behind my back and took a shot. "Hey, I thought you were just learning?!"

"I am, but I'm not that good. You should see some of these guys shoot pool at the club. Georgie Roderick is one of the best pool shooters in Stonington. These guys can make all kinds of shots. I was just giving it a try."

When it was time for the operation, Dr. Jones told me I would be in good hands with Dr. Elliot and that he would be seeing me most every day. Dr. Elliot explained to me what he was going to do. He would need to take a piece of bone from my hip. He drew a picture that looked like a little cradle, and that piece of bone was somehow grafted into the bone in my neck.

When I woke up from the operation, I couldn't move. I had a metal breast plate with leather close to my skin, strapped on my chest and back. I couldn't move by head because I had a metal chin rest and back neck support, which was attached to the body piece holding my head in place. If I wanted to move I had to turn my whole body. I don't ever recall taking it off for at least six or seven months.

I didn't go back to work for some time after that. Now, I understand, they perform that kind of operation and they only use a whiplash collar after the surgery. It's almost unbelievable. After that operation, I have never had a pain in my neck.

Swordfishing

One year we decided to do something different. During swordfishing season we asked everyone if they wanted to put up five dollars a man. Whoever got to catch the first fish of the season would get all the money. I, Jimmy Henry, got the first fish every year but one. The very last tournament we had Sterl, a local fisherman, who worked at Johnny Bindloss' hardware store. And he ran one of Bindloss' boats. Bindloss owned five or six boats at that time. Sterl fished for quite some time until he retired and he went to Key West.

I used to hear of the big boats in Gloucester that used to go swordfishing. Some of these boats were called eastern riggers because the wheelhouse is on the stern of the boat. They used to say they caught as many as ten to twenty fish in one stretch. I never believed them because none of us caught that many fish in one run.

The way we caught swordfish is once someone spots a fish he says, "Sword-fish!"

"Where is he?" asks the wheelman. The spotter tells him port or starboard until the wheelman sees the fish. Then everyone is quiet until the wheelman brings the boat as close as he can so the striker can strike the fish with his harpoon. When he strikes the fish, he throws a keg overboard, pulls in the pole and re-rigs it for the next throw. His part of the job is done.

On that day the striker, who was me, had 19 fish on 19 harpoon throws! As I looked forward, I saw swordfish as far as I could see. That's what made me be-lieve the Gloucester boats could catch that many. If I had known that, I would have brought 20 kegs or more!

After the strike, the dory man gets in the dory, rows over to the keg , grabs it and pulls the fish to the surface. He places a rope around its tail then raises an oar to signal the boat to come pick the fish up. Once the fish is on the deck of the big boat, we tow the dory man to the next keg. Meantime we've already hit another fish and dropped another keg. The fish is hauled into the big boat and its sword is removed so it won't damage other fish.

Sometimes it's the fish who damages the dory. Some years before, Herbie Clay from Mystic, was the dory man on The New England, owned by Alfred Rubello. Herbie lit a cigarette. He had a couple of puffs before putting his gloves back on to haul the fish. As he was hauling the rope, the swordfish, which was coming up faster than he could pull the rope, shot through the bottom of the dory, which began to fill with water. He put his oar up. When we got to dory he was lying flat on his stomach, still holding the the fish's sword. He wasn't going to let it go! Once we saw what was happening, we pulled him off the dory, then got the fish and the dory onto the deck. We cleaned the hull and applied a fiberglass patch and allowed the dory to dry while we looked for more fish.

This happened many years before. On this trip, we started the whole thing over again looking for more fish, only this time we circled the dory, but kept an eye on the man at all times. That day, we caught 18 more fish with only six kegs at a time – that's all I had! We debated on whether to stay and fish – I'd never had 19 swordfish on any trip. We decided we'd get a better price if we went in early before the other boats got in with their catches and drove the price of swordfish down. Of course I went to New Bedford and sold my catch to Tommy Aiello!

Doctor Holiday

We went fishing off Block Island. About two hours off Block Island we set the net. After about twenty minutes, the cook said "OK, Captain, breakfast is on the table. I went down and sat at the table, took one bite, and felt something in my stomach. I had an idea it was my ulcers but I wasn't sure. So I went up to the wheelhouse again and I called Denny Cidel on the boat Carolyn Dennis. I asked him to give Doctor Holiday a call and explain what was wrong. Doctor Holiday told Denny to tell me to come right in. He said, "I will have the ambulance at the dock waiting for you and he will meet me at the hospital."

When I got to the Westerly Hospital, they examined me and told Doctor Holiday that it was my ulcers and they were going to start treating me. Doctor

Holiday said he wanted me to go to Boston because I had these ulcers for a long time and he felt I should have part of my stomach removed. He told me he arranged it with the government and they decided to go to the Brighton Marine Hospital for Seamen.

While I was there I met three other fishermen from Gloucester . I didn't know what they were there for, but they were with their wives. I was there for two or three months and on the third month I said to the doctor, "Hey, what's going on here, anyways?" He said he was treating me. I said I didn't want to be treated because if I didn't have a fast boat I would be dead. He said they were having a consultation about all the patients and he would bring my case up and see if there was anything they could do.

When he came back to me he said they were going to operate on me! It just so happened that that was the time when they were going to make a movie and all the doctors and nurses were going to be in it. I don't know why they were making the movie – I just know they were making it.

The nurse that was taking care of me wasn't supposed to leave that room. She was supposed to keep an eye on me and the pump they had me hooked up to. But at that time I was feeling good. Another nurse came by and she asked me

"Do you mind if this nurse stays with you till I get back? I will not take long." When she came back, she saw my face in a lot of pain and she noticed the pump was clogged so she freed the pump and I came back to normal.

When the movie was completed they played it for the hospital. The nurses were some disappointed because they had taken all the nurses in the movie out and replaced them with other people.

After the operation, I saw some pictures of how they did it. I said if I had known how they did it, I would never have had that operation! They open you up like a pig and they put sticks across to keep you open so they can keep working on you – that's what it looked like to me. When it was over, they had taken two-thirds of my stomach out. I don't remember how long I stood there – it had to be at least a month or month and a half. All I know is I couldn't go fishing for about eight months or so.

Towing for Scup

When I first became captain I did not know much about nets. We were fishing and I ripped a net. This was off Watch Hill Lighthouse. We had to use landmarks not to rip but I did. I called George Roderick and I said I am going in– I ripped up bad. He said, "Come and pick me up. I will fix the net so you can fish the rest of the day."

Over the years as I was fishing and every time one of the boys that fished with us and they had plumbing problems at their house. "Who can I get?– call Jimmy, call Jimmy." – but I was rewarded too – every time I ripped a net –a lot of work involved and they'd all jump in and help me fix the net so I could go fishing with them at the same time.

We dragged for scup, the kind of fish when you take the net in the bag floats before the boards come out of the water. If we see the boards come out and the bag is floating we got fish! One man goes below to ice the pens. We then bring the boards in. Some of the net stays in the water so we can move the fish away from the bag so when we put the hook to lift the bag of fish and put it on deck. We then open the bottom of the bag to let the fish out, then we open the deck plate to put the fish, then put ice over the fish to keep the fish cool. We keep doing that until all the fish is in the pens. We try to keep the weight between four and five thousand pounds so as not to crush the fish. That kind of fish, sometimes we get so much fish we let some go.

My Perfect Storm

I was talking to George Roderick about scup and he said, "This is the right time of the year that we fishermen go looking for scup." I told him that the price should be good if we get them. "I think that if you or I get them, we should not say we got them. Too many boats are fishing here - if all the boats go fishing for scup the price will drop."

I made a short tow for a half hour – I got a sign of scup. "I'm going to make one more tow!" I said. Georgie said, "I'm going home. All the boats are going home, even the big boats are going home." I asked my crew, "What do you think - shall we make one more tow? Yes or no?"

"We came together with Georgie – we should go home together with Georgie," they said. I told them to put the canvas over the hatch and nail it.

Now I'm glad they said that, even though I wanted to make one more tow, because we wouldn't be here today. I was going northeast for about one hour when I realized I was going too close to Montauk Point. The water is awfully rough there as a rule; that's when I decided to go a few more degrees to the east because I figured I'd had more of a chance getting in deeper water.

I had shoal water to my left. I had shoal water to my right. And I had shoal water ahead of me. I thought I would be better off going this way instead of going to Montauk Point where I might have had the lee of the land but I wasn't sure. I hadn't spoken to George since we decided to go in. I was on my own and was trying to make the best decision. I didn't know then if I had made the correct decision, but I'm alive now, and what happened next could have killed us.

A big sea came and I tell you it was a big sea. The *Perfect Storm* comes to mind. The *New England* was sixty foot-long. We held it wide open as we climbed the wave and I thought we were going to slide back because I didn't think the motor had enough power to get me over that wave. We got to the top of the wave and over the top and we came right down like a kid on a sled going down a really steep hill. As we went down that hill we didn't say one word to one another. All we did is hold our breath. When we hit the bottom of that wave, the boat went right under water. I thought with the way the boat hit the water and the sound that it made that it was going to burst into pieces. The three of us stood in the wheelhouse very surprised that even the windows didn't break.

Before we even had a chance to realize what had happened, the second wave came – just as big as the first one! We were coming down on the second wave just like we rode the first, but this time when we hit the bottom, the boat rolled to the port side and the mast went into the water.

Now, when I first took on the boat, it didn't have any ballast. We would haul a bag of fish in that could weigh five thousand pounds or more. The boat would list and we couldn't put the bag where we wanted. We had to put another block on the side rigging to pull the bag to the middle of the boat and use another rope and hook to the other drum so we could bring the bag to just where we wanted to dump it.

Once the bag comes out of the water, the whip holds the net up. Next, we put a strap around the bag, and we put the block and falls onto the strap. Then we put a strain on there and let the whip go. The block and falls take care of the weight and you can go and raise the bag up and put it on the deck. But the boat can take a list if the bag is real heavy. Once you get the weight of that on the block and falls, you can take the whip off. Then you put the whip by the other block that's got the bag. Next, you put a strain on the whip to bring the bag where you want to dump the fish. The bag is then in its place. But that takes time, time we needed. I had been having trouble with moving that bag where we wanted. It was taking too much time using that block so I told the owner, Mr. Rubella, what I thought I needed there.

He said, "Capin' Zshimmy, when this boat is tied to the dock, it's my boat. When you take the boat out, it's your boat. You do what you think has gotta be done."

So I told him I was going to put cement down by the keel to steady it. I put so damn much cement in the keel and back near the ice box in the stern that everyone thought I had a load of fish. I put so much cement there that I blocked the air space and the boat stunk. When I would go to New Bedford I would get Wally Piver to lump the fish and he would bring his wife down with the chemicals to get that smell out. If I didn't have all that cement in there, the boat would have sunk coming down off that wave. That cement brought that boat right back where it belonged. We were so scared we wouldn't say, "Shit!" if we had a mouthful.

After we tied up I went to see Mr. Rubella and told him what happened. When he came down to the dock to see the boat, he said to me, "Cap'in Zhimmy, when you come to my house I don' believe you, but I believe you now - I see you." He saw me trying to dry the charts!

I'm not sure how long it really was, but it seemed like within ten to fifteen minutes. The seas calmed down and the water was about as flat as the floor. I'm not actually sure I spoke the words or not – but I thought it was a miracle! I thank God for our lives.

Academy

When I came to the Academy I was lost. I sat at a table with three women. They were talking . The woman to my left said, "I will spend twenty dollars; I will go for the boat ride."

I said, "I've been in too many boats – I have seen so much water that I'd like to stay dry." But when I got home I said, "I haven't been on a steamboat, maybe I should go just to see what it looks like."

The bus driver took us from home to the dock. We got on the boat. Tony brought some lunch and she gave each one of us a box of lunch. When the boat left the dock, I said to Therese Portelance, "Do you mind if I stay on this side of the boat because I can see better? I will tell you as much as I can about it - like this is Abbott's Lobsters. This is a good place to eat. Before I sold my lobster boat, The *Noranda*, I took my wife, Claire Smith and Claire's friend for a boat ride."

We went all the way up the river until we got to the train tracks and then we turned around but I said, "My granddaughters have boats alike – maybe we will see them. Look, that's Marlisa, we can go some day for a ride with them. We can bring our lunch and spend part of the day with them, if you like to do something like that or stop at Abbott's Lobsters." Therese said "I would like that."

Therese has been a big help to me whenever I got to a point that I didn't know just what to do or say. "I am not going to say another word. You can do this, I know you can," Teri would say. Once or twice she spelled something but after that, she refused to help. "I know you can do it." When I told her that she said, "You can do that – I know you can do that" – thereafter, I had to do it on my own. She said that I was sort of depending on her to help me when I was stuck.

"From now on," she said, " that's it! You've got to learn how to spell it and you've got to learn how to write it. This is your story; it's not mine." She doesn't think she's done anything special. She never had to go through what I did, I didn't start really learning to read and write until I came to the Academy where I met her and I appreciate everything she has done for me.

I had told my granddaughters, if I came to the Academy and if had the time, I would learn to read and write. "Gee, that's good, Pop," Marlisa said. My grandchildren bought me two books: *Life is so Good*, by George Dawson and Richard Glaubman and *Healthy at 100* by John Robbins. Dawson, who could not read or write like me finally learned how, got educated and became a teacher himself. Like me, he had people to help him.

I owe so much to Marlisa and my other granddaughter, Alicia, as well as to my Literacy Volunteer tutor, Mark Hogan. I don't know how to thank them enough for all the help they have given me. I don't know how I could have jumped over that fence without their help.

North Star

I was down on the patio here at the Academy. Everybody was so quiet and everything. I turned around to one of my friends and said, "Gee it's pretty quiet here. No one's talking. I think I'll tell a story and see if I can get people to liven up a little bit."

I spoke up and asked them for their attention for a moment. I told them I had something I wanted to share with them.

"Me being a fisherman, I know that lots of you people don't know what we go through at times, but with my experience I would like to have you know just what happens now and then."

Everybody looked up and listened. Nobody said anything. "We were fishing in ninety to a hundred fathom. Now that's way out in deep water. We were on two nights and three days fishing -around the clock- we don't stop. The only time we get some sleep is in between when we set the net and haul the net. One man stays at the wheel and three go down to sleep. The man at the wheel runs his shift for the hour and a half while the others sleep, until the wheel man wakes us up."

I was asleep when the wheel man came rushing down and woke us all up and says, "Cap!! It's thick of fog out there and something's wrong. The towing cable is out in front of us instead of behind us."

I looked around. All the people were looking nervous like. I continued. "So I says, 'It's got to be a submarine that hooked on to us and is towing us out into deeper water!' "

"I ran right up on deck to check things out. 'Right now I don't know where we're at because I can't find bottom with the fathometer. The fog's shut in so tight I can't see the stars, either…..I'm lost. Right now I don't know where we're at.'"

They were all at the edge of their seat like. "Just then the towing cable parted and the boat slowed down. 'I just hope we have enough fuel to get home because I don't know just how far we've been dragged.'"

"Then the fog cleared up and I saw the stars, and I saw the North Star, so I told the fellas, I says, 'Don't worry fellas. I know exactly where we're at and we're not lost!'

"And I knew right where I was. And I was right in bed. Dreaming!"

DEAR BOBBY,

THIS IS YOUR UNCLE JIM,
I KNOW THAT YOU MUST HAVE
THOUGHT I FORGOT ALL
ABOUT YOU BUT I WOULD
LIKE TO THANK YOU. I COULD
NEVER FORGET YOU BECAUSE
OF THE WAY YOU SAID TO ME
THAT YOU WOULD NOT TAKE A
PHONE CALL FROM ME. I
KNOW YOU MEANT WELL. YOU
GAVE ME THE AMBITION TO
ANSWER YOU. AND I THANK YOU.
I WILL TRY MY BEST TO PLEASE
ALL OF YOU THAT ARE HELPING
ME I THANK YOU ALL. J.H.

"Don't call me - I won't answer. Write me a letter instead..."

In order to encourage his uncle to learn to read and write, Bob told Jim the next time he wanted to communicate it had to be in the form of a letter.